I Can Write My ABC's
Mini-Books

by Kama Einhorn

SCHOLASTIC
PROFESSIONAL BOOKS

New York • Toronto • London • Auckland • Sydney • Mexico City •
New Delhi • Hong Kong • Buenos Aires

For Eric Keitel, who makes friendship easy as ABC.

Acknowledgments

Grateful thanks to Liza Charlesworth and Terry Cooper for their editorial consideration and guidance, to my thoughtful editor Danielle Blood, and to all my colleagues at Professional Books, who make coming to work every morning a true pleasure.

Cover design by Jim Sarfati

Cover and interior illustrations by Steve Cox

Interior design by Ellen Matlach Hassell
for Boultinghouse & Boultinghouse, Inc.

ISBN: 0-439-22845-X

Copyright © 2001 by Kama Einhorn

Contents

Introduction

Welcome to *I Can Write My ABC's: Mini-Books*

What would we do without letters? Together, these 26 abstract symbols can work in endless combinations to represent any idea a human might have. Forming and recognizing letters is the most basic building block in a child's early literacy development.

When children are comfortable forming letters on paper and realize that their letters are recognizable to another reader—that their writing communicates the intended message—they have taken an important step in their development as writers. And when they can quickly recognize the letters that others have written, they can free up their mental energy for higher-level thinking rather than having to focus on decoding the sounds of individual letters.

Learning and practicing letter formation can be easy, creative, and fun! Help your students enjoy putting pencil to paper, and you will provide a solid foundation for the entire writing process.

Using the Mini-Books in Your Classroom

These 26 make-your-own mini-books are a great way to:

- introduce each letter.
- highlight a "letter of the week."
- help children focus on forming individual letters.
- give extra support and practice to children with learning challenges and small-motor limitations.
- enrich your writing center.
- build children's "book knowledge" (books have covers, we read from left to right, and so on).
- develop awareness of sound-symbol correspondence and relate it to letter formation.
- combine rote letter practice with creative thinking.
- provide individual children with independent work.
- reinforce recently learned letters.
- enrich children's writing portfolios.
- help children feel a sense of completion and mastery in a short period of time.

To make the mini-books, simply follow these steps:

1. Carefully remove the perforated page from the book.

2. Make a double-sided copy of the page on standard 8½- by 11-inch paper. (If your machine does not have a double-sided function, make single-sided copies. Cut along the dotted line, arrange the pages in order, and staple along the left side.)

3. Fold the page along the dotted line.

4. Distribute pencils and crayons, and guide children as they complete their books.

The Cover

Have children decorate the mini-book cover, coloring the letters, illustrations, and background. Then have them write their names on the "by" line at the bottom of the page. Together, look at the two-line mnemonic rhymes. These short rhymes give children auditory cues for forming each letter. Read the rhyme aloud to the group, pointing out the letter's formation. Ask children to finger-trace the letters on the cover as you read the rhyme for a second time. You might ask a child whose name begins with or includes that letter to demonstrate it on the board. Show children how to use the numbered arrows on the model letters as a guide.

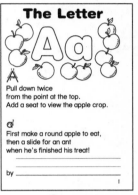

Cover

The Letter Practice Sheet

Rote letter practice plays an important role in learning letter formation. The process of printing each letter helps children integrate it into their muscle memory, ultimately making letter formation second nature. Letter practice also helps children combine the visual image of the letter with the motor movement involved in writing it.

These letter practice pages feature write-on lines for children to practice each upper- and lowercase letter. The model letters include numbered arrows to show the direction and order of the strokes to form each letter. A letter at the end of each line ensures that left-handed children can see the model as they practice. Draw children's attention to the dots on the write-on lines. Explain that they should place the point of their pencil on the dot to begin writing the first letter.

Letter Practice Page

When helping children practice letter formation, follow these simple steps for each upper- and lowercase letter:

- First, preview the letter before having children write it. Slowly demonstrate the letter on the board as you say the rhyme out loud.

- Next, have students air trace the letter as you read the rhyme again, holding their thumb and first two fingers together (as if they were holding a pencil) and forming the letter in the air.

Color each apple with an **a** inside.

3

Letter Activity Page

Here are things that begin with **Aa**!

4

Sound-Symbol Page

• Then, ask students to pick up their pencils and write one letter on their page. Circulate around the room and check to see that all students have understood the basic strokes. If they haven't, take their hand in yours and guide it through the strokes. Invite them to complete two rows of the letter and then circle their best letter.

• Last, have children form their best lower- and uppercase letters in the frames at the bottom of the page.

The Letter Activity Page

These pages feature interactive exercises that combine letter formation, letter recognition, sound-symbol correspondence, and creative thinking. Help children get started on these pages before they complete them independently. Read the instructions together and brainstorm ideas if necessary.

The Sound-Symbol Page

Children can complete the last page in several ways. You might brainstorm ideas as a group before children get started. Here are some suggestions. Invite children to:

• draw things that begin with the featured letter.

• draw a large letter made up of something that begins with that letter—for example, an *A* made of apples or a *B* made of blueberries.

• clip pictures of objects that begin with the letter from old magazines and glue the pictures onto the page.

• write words that begin with the letter. (Encourage children to include the names of classmates whenever possible.)

Consider children's skill levels as you introduce this page. For example, you may want younger children to clip pictures, while older children write words.

When children have completed their mini-books, they might:

• take the books home and share them with their families.

• share the books with their younger siblings or with younger children in your school.

• share their art from the activity pages with the rest of the class.

• store the books in an "alphabet folder" that will eventually hold all 26 mini-books.

• add the books to the class library corner.

On pages 59–62, you'll find a longer mini-book entitled "I Can Write My ABC's!" After children have completed all 26 letter mini-books, they can review the entire alphabet with this alphabet mini-book. Refer to pages 63–64 for suggested alphabet books that children will enjoy. Happy reading and writing!

The Letter

Pull down twice
from the point at the top.
Add a seat to view the apple crop.

First make a round apple to eat,
then a slide for an ant
when he's finished his treat!

by _____

I Can Write My ABCs: Mini-Books   Scholastic Professional Books

Here are things that begin with **Aa**!

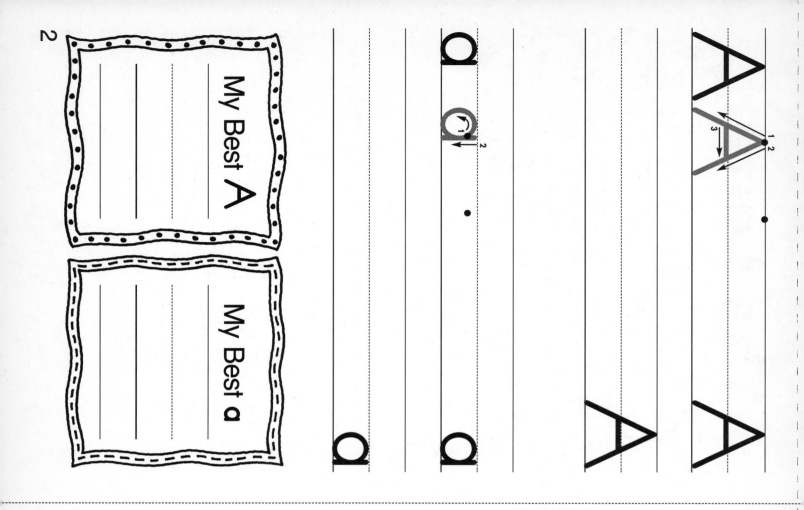

My Best A

My Best a

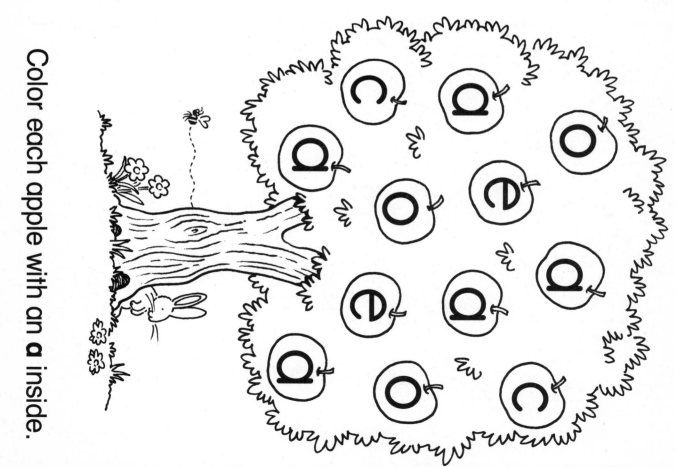

Color each apple with an **a** inside.

The Letter

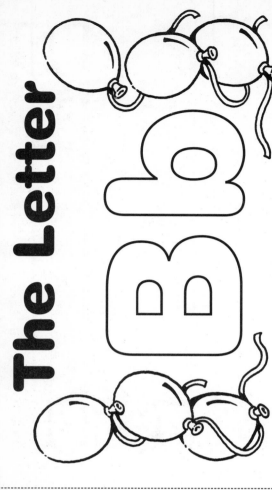

B b

Big old **B** has a tall straight back,
and two big bellies,
'cause he just ate a snack!

Draw a straight back, just like me.
Don't forget to add a belly for **b**!

by _____

1

Here are things that begin with **Bb**!

4

B B

b

b

b

b

B B

B B

My Best B

My Best b

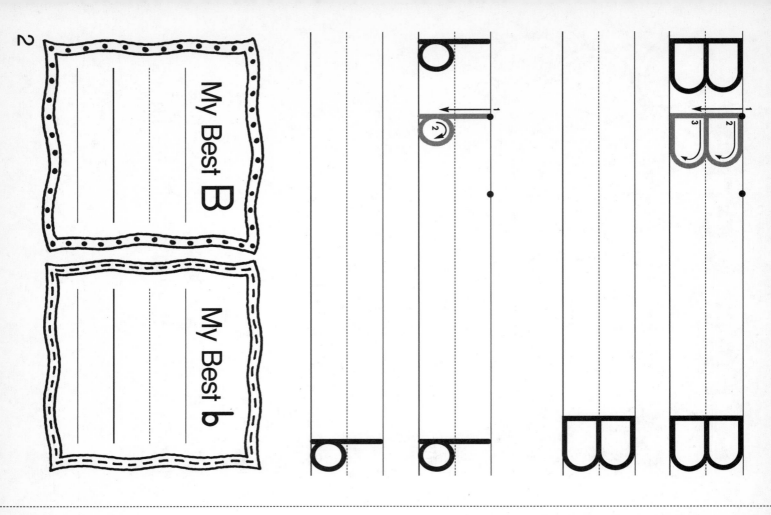

Write **B** or **b** in each letter block.
Then color your blocks.

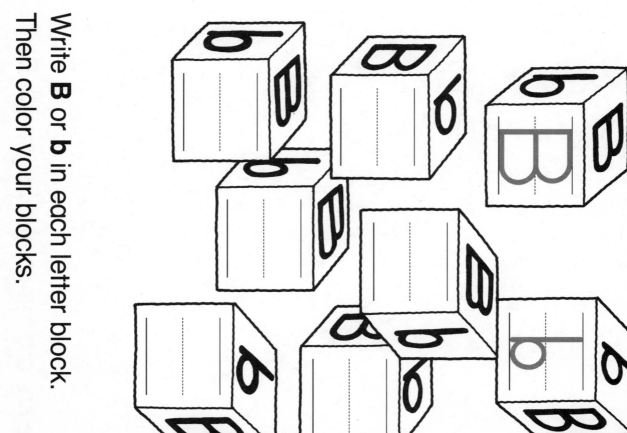

The Letter

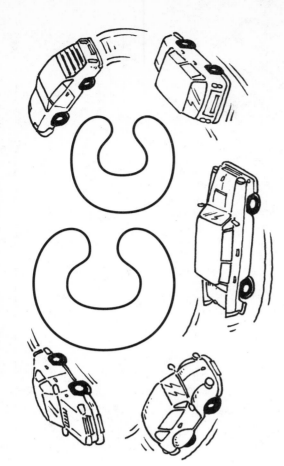

C c

Cars can cruise down curvy **c**.
Stop near the ground—
that's it, you see!

by _____

I Can Write My ABCs: Mini-Books   Scholastic Professional Books

Here are things that begin with **Cc**!

My Best C

My Best c

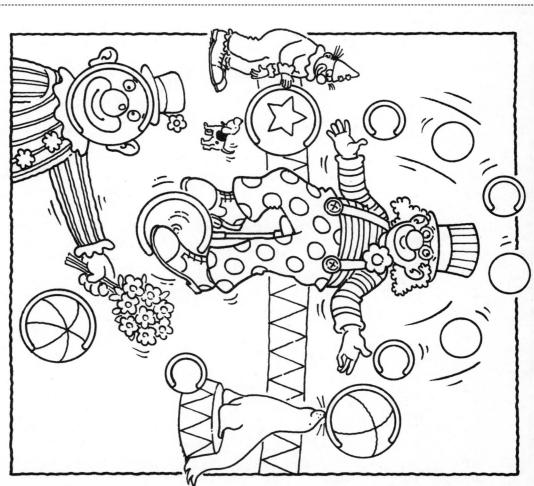

How many **Cc**'s are
in this clown's circus?
Circle them all.
Then color the circus.

The Letter Dd

Down to the ground,
then take a break.
Half a circle is what you'll make.

First you make a dime to spend.
Go way up high,
then down to the end.

by _____

1

Here are things that begin with **Dd!**

4

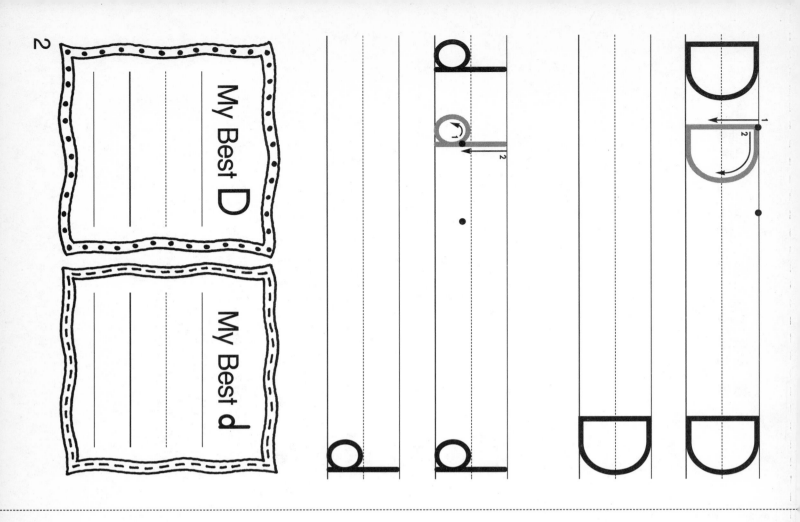

My Best D

My Best d

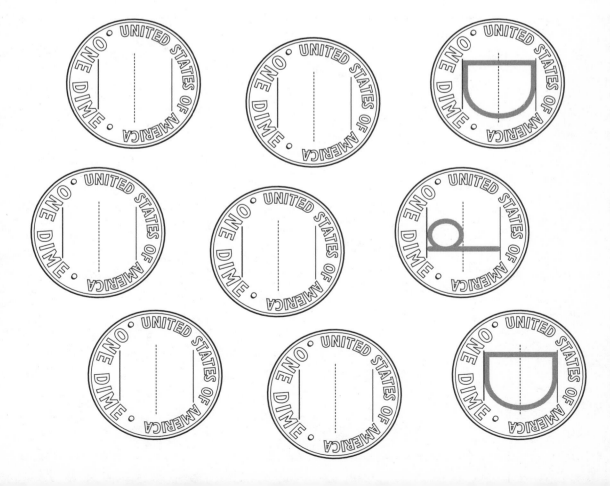

Write a **D** or **d** on each dime.
Then color the dimes.

The Letter Ee

Pull straight down for capital E.
Then add some shelves, 1, 2, 3.

A little line starts off e.
Add a plate for an egg—
here's breakfast for me!

by _____

I Can Write My ABCs: Mini-Books   Scholastic Professional Books

Here are things that begin with Ee!

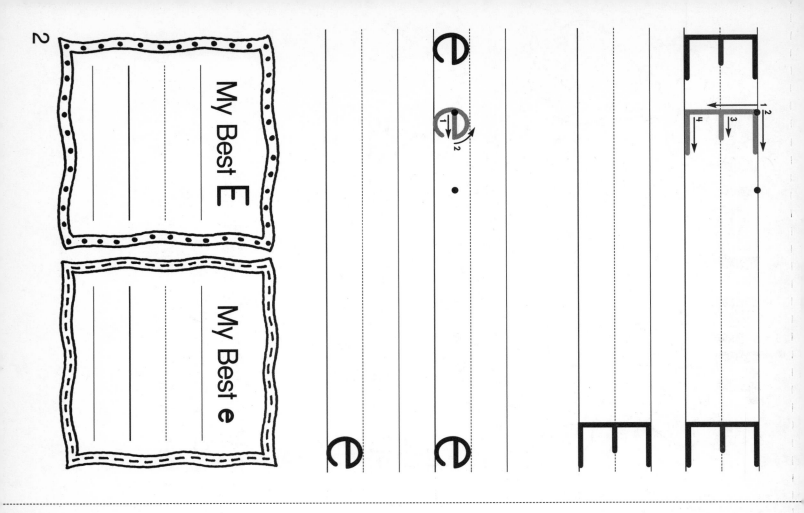

My Best E

My Best e

e e

e e

E E

E E

Color the eggs with **E** or **e**.

F F e
o e E H
E o E H c
a H e F

The Letter Ff

Big **F** is a tall flower for you.
F has three lines, **F** has two.

This flower grows tall
and hangs a little.
Add a line right in the middle.

I Can Write My ABCs: Mini-Books   Scholastic Professional Books

by _____

Here are things that begin with **Ff**!

My Best F

My Best f

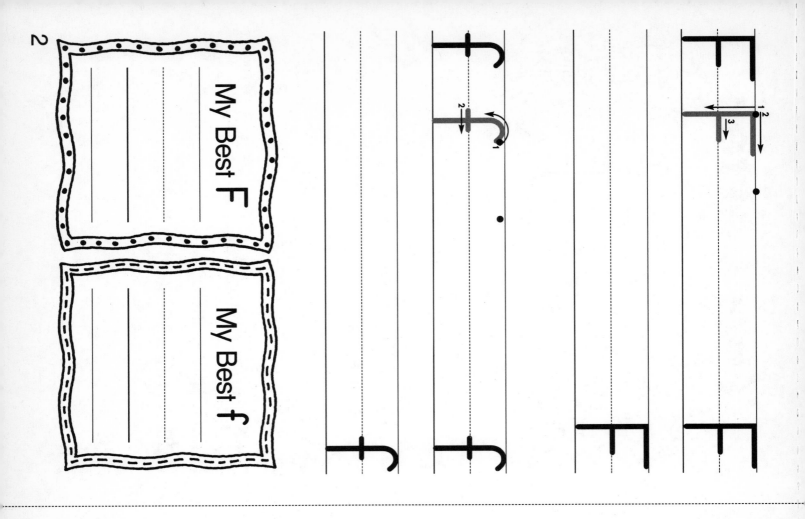

Color the **F** in this flag.
Then color your flag however you like.

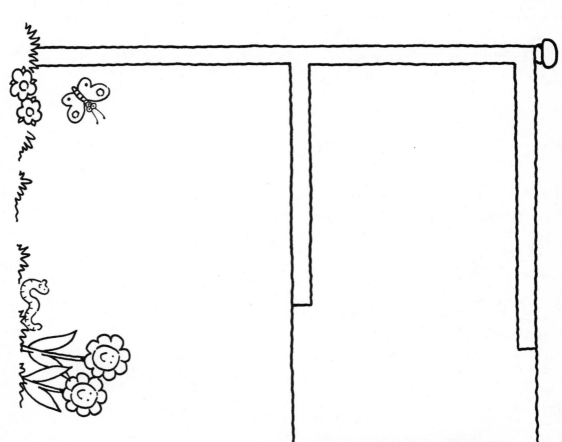

The Letter Gg

Big round circle, but don't go too far.
Add a garage to park your car!

g

A garden starts with a little seed.
The roots grow down.
That's all you need!

by _____

1

Here are things that begin with **Gg!**

4

G G G G

g g

g g g g

My Best G

My Best g

Help this garden grow!
Circle all the **Gg**'s.
Then color the garden.

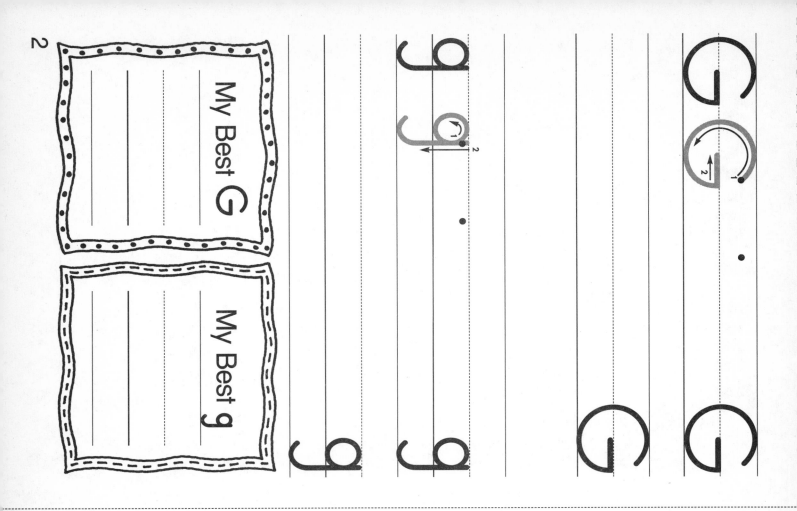

The Letter Hh

Make two lines, high to low.
Connect the lines
so they can say hello!

First start high, then take a jump.
Little **h** has a little hump.

by _____

1

Here are things that begin with **Hh**!

4

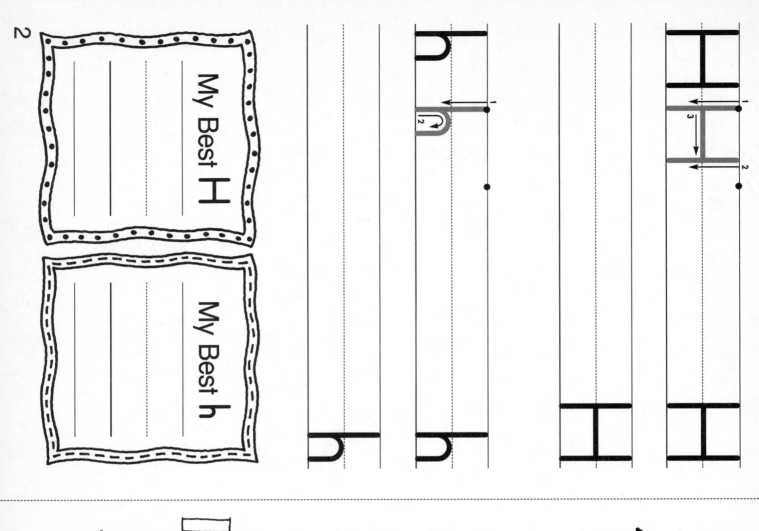

My Best H

My Best h

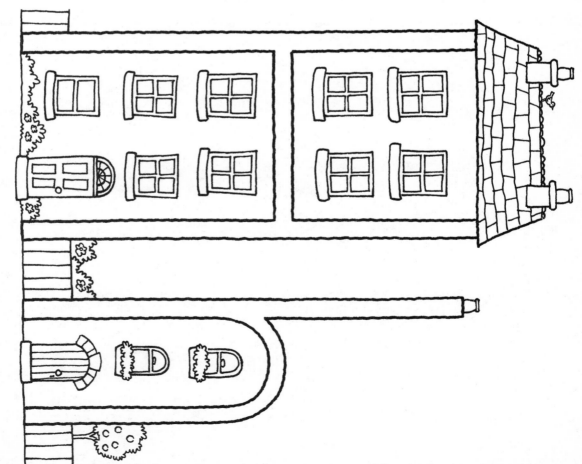

Use crayons to color **H** and **h**.
Then color the houses.

The Letter

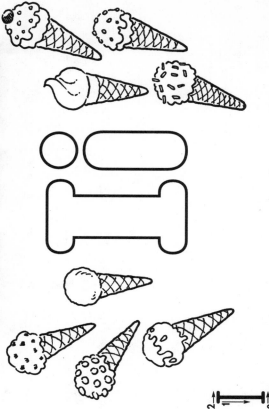

Ii

Big **I** starts with one side of a door.
All it needs is a roof and a floor.

Little i goes down.
It's an ice cream treat.
Add a sprinkle on top,
and it's ready to eat!

by _____

I Can Write My ABCs: Mini-Books   Scholastic Professional Books

Here are things that begin with **Ii!**

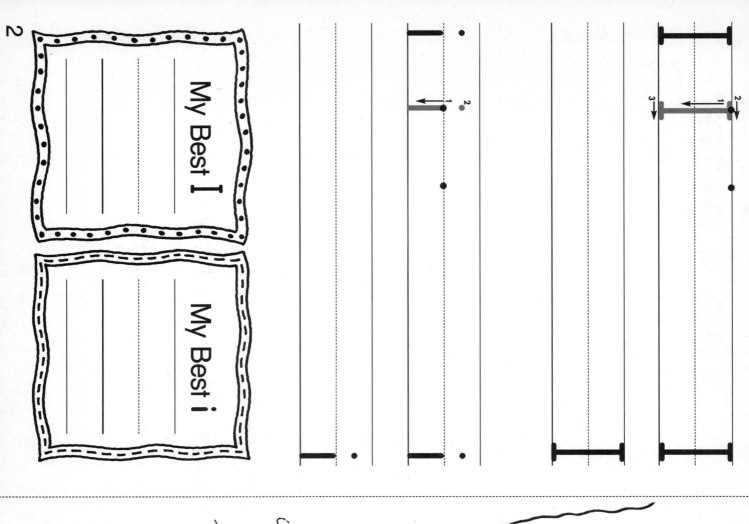

My Best I

My Best i

Write **I**'s in the big icicles.
Write i's in the little icicles.

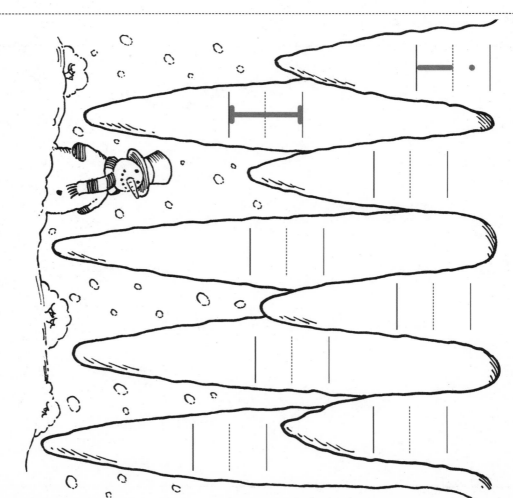

The Letter Jj

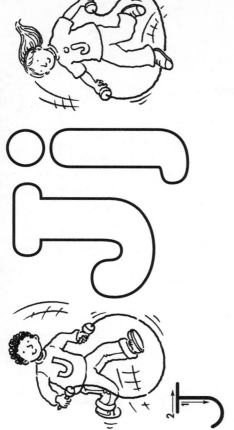

Jumping Jack **J**
jumps down and then curls up.
Jack needs a hat
'cause he likes to dress up!

Little **j** is so thin and lean.
Jump way down,
then add a jelly bean!

by _____

I Can Write My ABCs: Mini-Books   Scholastic Professional Books

Here are things that begin with **Jj**!

My Best J

My Best j

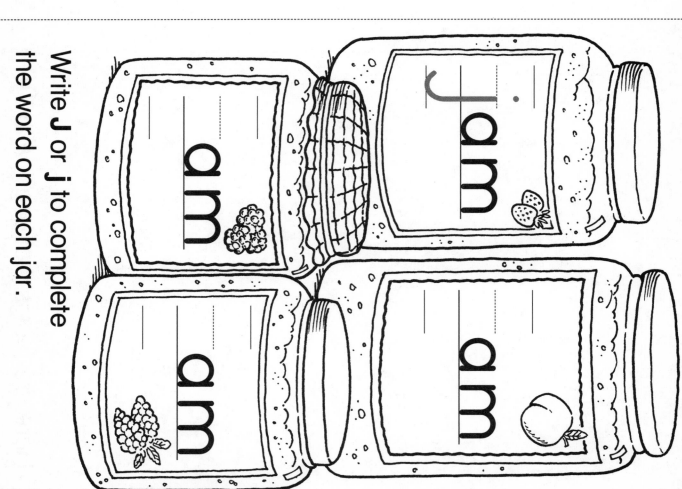

Write J or j to complete
the word on each jar.

jam

am

am

am

The Letter

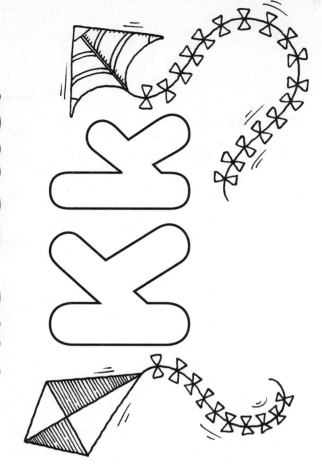

K and **k** have three lines,
as you can see:
a tall, straight back,
and a sideways v.

by _____

I Can Write My ABCs: Mini-Books   Scholastic Professional Books

Here are things that begin with **Kk!**

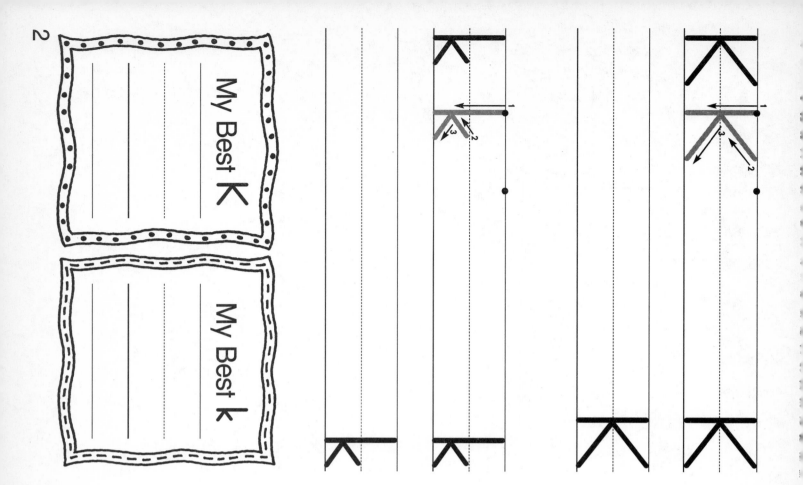

My Best K

My Best k

What kinds of animals are in Australia? Write **K** or **k** on the lines to find out. Then draw the animals on the postcards.

angaroo

oala

The Letter Ll

Pull down a line and add a lap.
Lie down, lazy! It's time for a nap!

Little l looks like number one.
Just draw a line and you are done!

by _____

I Can Write My ABCs: Mini-Books Scholastic Professional Books

Here are things that begin with **Ll**!

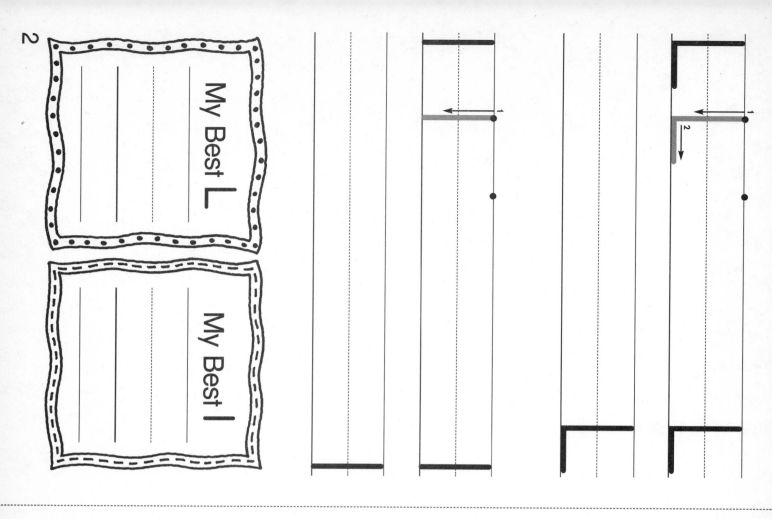

My Best L

My Best l

Write **L** or **l** on each lollipop.
Then color the lollipops.

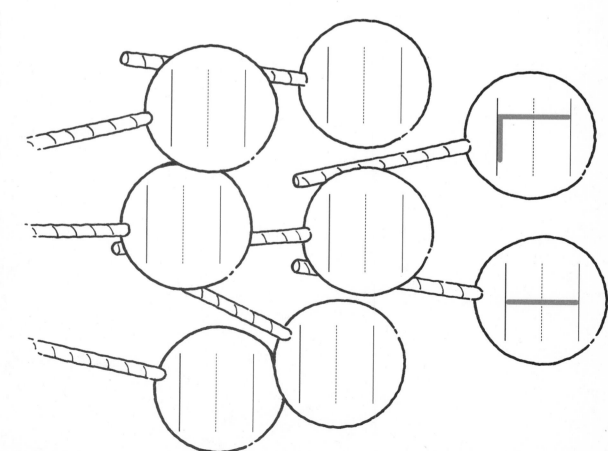

The Letter Mm

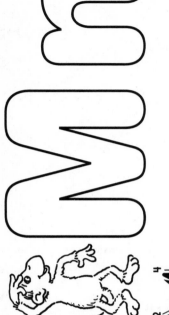

Go down, hit the ground,
then draw a V.
Down to the ground again,
big **M** is two mountains for me.

Go down, hit the ground,
then get ready for bumps.
Little **m** is easy to write,
just add two humps.

I Can Write My ABCs: Mini-Books   Scholastic Professional Books

by _____

Here are things that begin with **Mm**!

My Best M

My Best m

M N

M

M

m m

m

m

Draw a moon.
Then color the mountains.

The Letter

Nn

${}^1_\rightarrow\!N\!{}^2_3$

Stick a nail in the ground,
slant another one right.
Add a third pointing up,
and say nighty-night!

${}^1n\,{}^2$

Go down, hit the ground,
and you're almost done.
Little m has two humps,
little n has one.

by _____

I Can Write My ABCs: Mini-Books   Scholastic Professional Books

Here are things that begin with **Nn!**

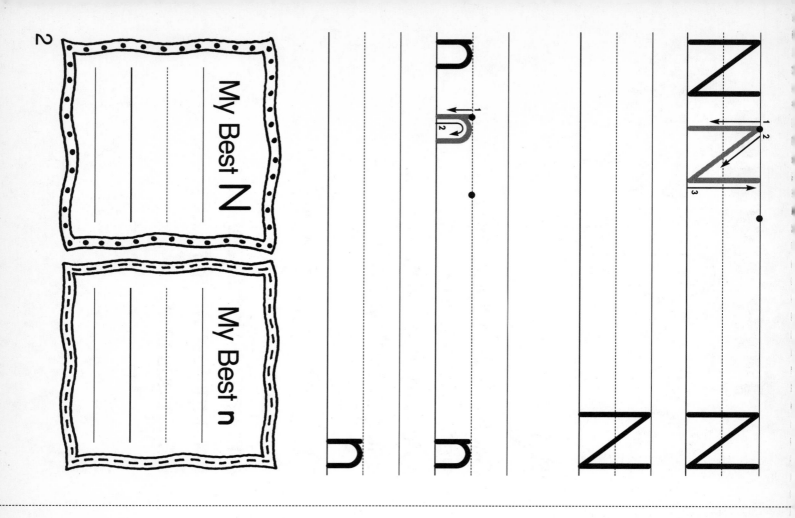

My Best N

My Best n

---

n   m   w   n

h   u   m   n

M   N   V

W   V   N

Circle all the Nn's in the newspaper.

The Letter

Oo

Oh, yum! An orange to eat!
Nice and round,
it's a healthy treat.

by _____

I Can Write My ABCs: Mini-Books   Scholastic Professional Books

Here are things that begin with **Oo**!

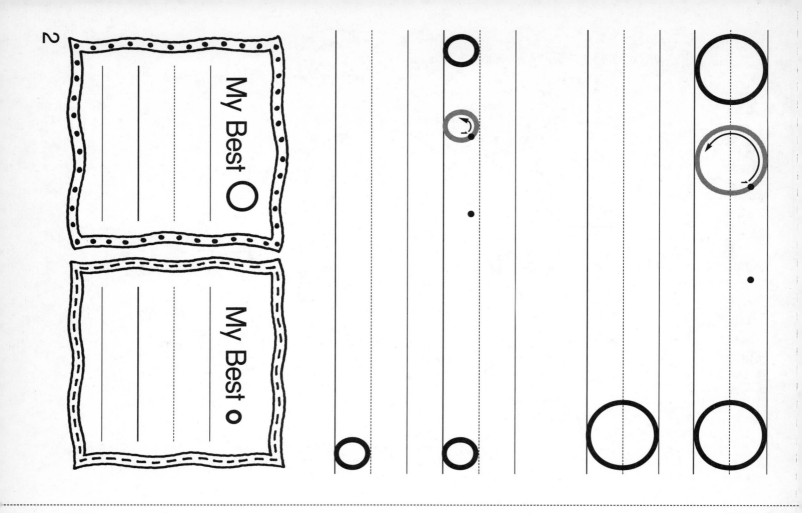

My Best O

My Best o

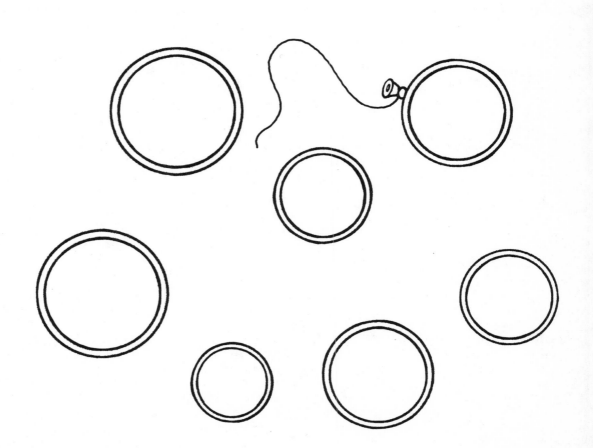

Turn all the **Oo**'s into things that are round.

The Letter Pp

Pull down your pencil,
then pick it up off the ground.
Add half a penny, nice and round.

Pop on down and then up, you see.
Finish it off with a little pea!

by _____

I Can Write My ABCs: Mini-Books   Scholastic Professional Books

Here are things that begin with **Pp**!

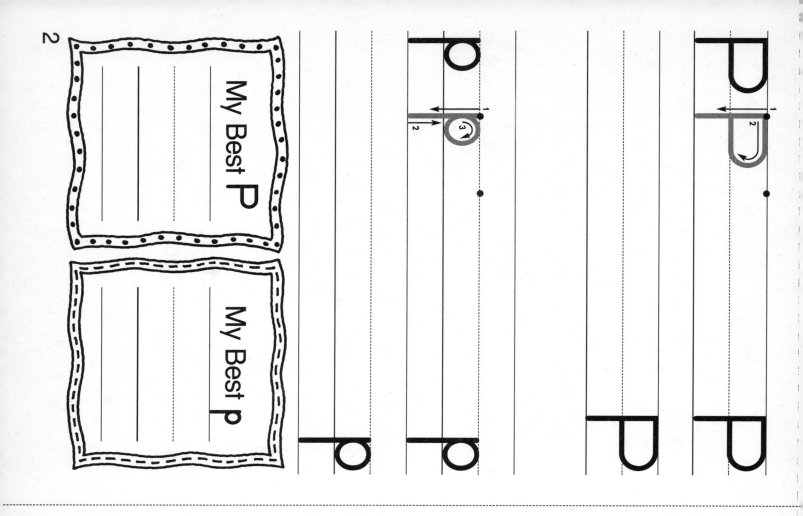

My Best P

My Best p

Draw a pretty picture of **P** and **p**.

The Letter

Big **Q** is a round quarter to spend.
Add a line when you're at the end.

A fancy queen with a little pearl.
Give **q**'s hair a special curl.

by _____

1

Here are things that begin with **Qq!**

4

My Best Q

My Best q

Color the q squares one color.
Color the other squares a
different color.

The Letter Rr

First draw a line and then a rainbow.
Add a ramp and you're ready to go!

Go straight down, then race on back.
r has an arm, like a little rack.

by _____

1

Here are things that begin with **Rr**!

4

My Best R

My Best r

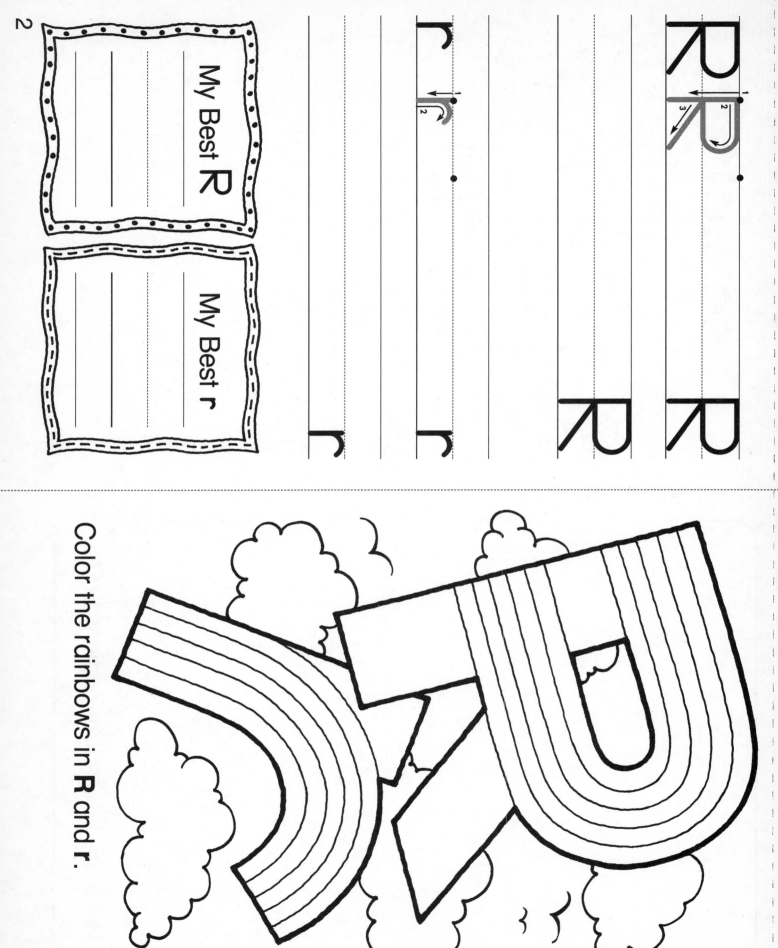

Color the rainbows in **R** and **r**.

The Letter

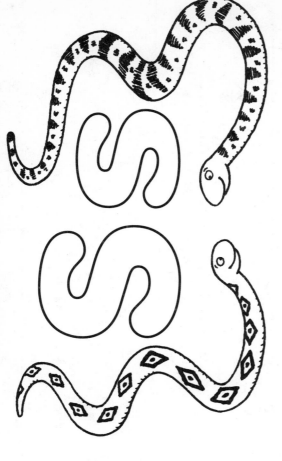

Ss

Silly **S** and **s**, those slithery snakes.
Twisty, turny, ready to shake!

by _____

1

Here are things that begin with **Ss!**

4

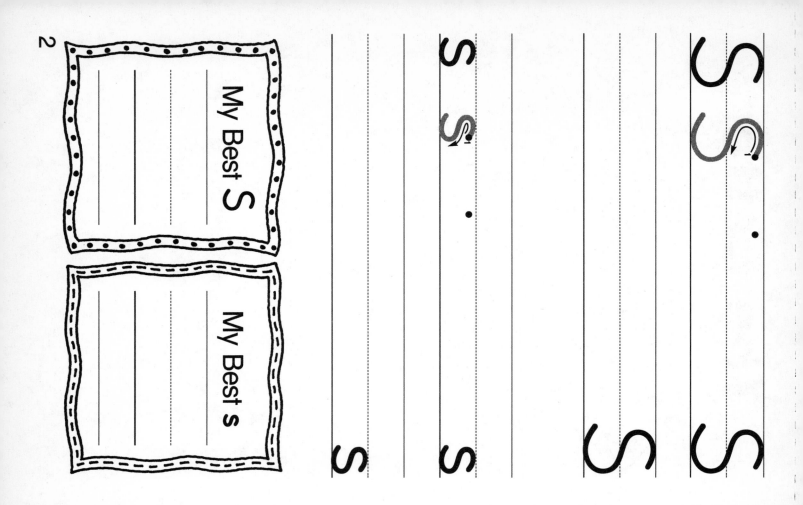

S s

My Best S

My Best s

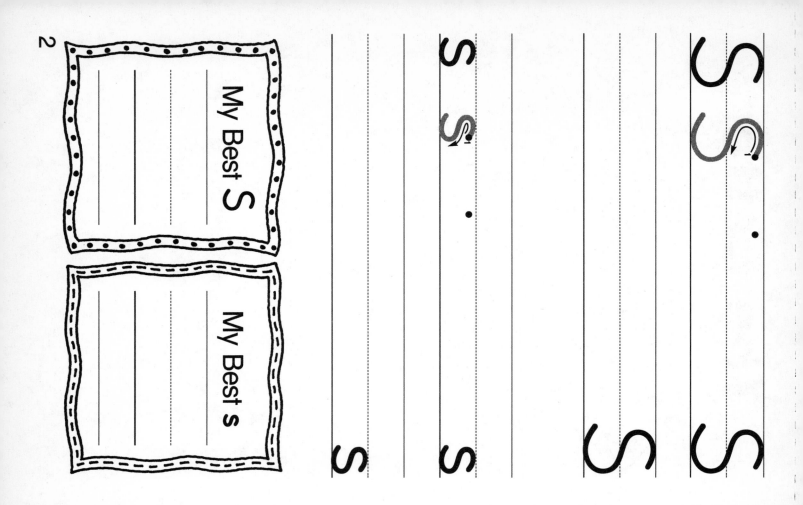

Trace **S** and **s**.
Then design your own **Ss** stamp.

Ss

The Letter Tt

Big **T** is a big tall tree.
Add a fort at the top so you can see.

Little **t** is a little tree.
Add a fort in the middle
for you and me!

by _____

1

Here are things that begin with **Tt**!

4

My Best T

My Best t

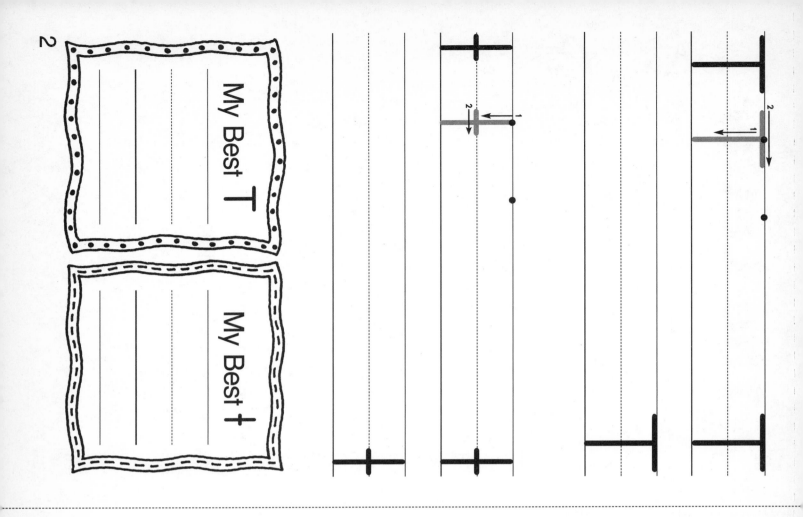

Turn T and t into trees!
Use crayons to add leaves.

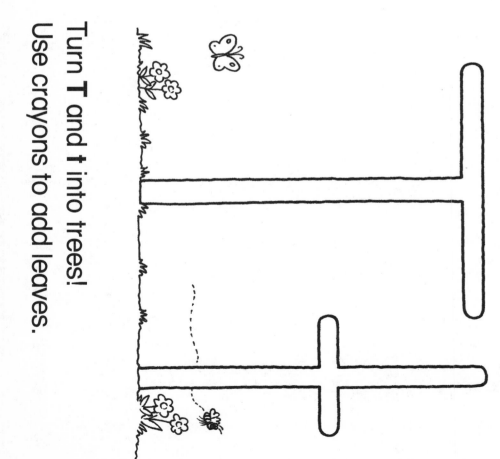

The Letter

Big **U** is just like a cup.
Start by going down,
and then curve up.

u²
↓

Curve down and up,
then down once more.
Little **u** is a cup that's ready to pour.

by _____

I Can Write My ABCs: Mini-Books   Scholastic Professional Books

Here are things that begin with **Uu!**

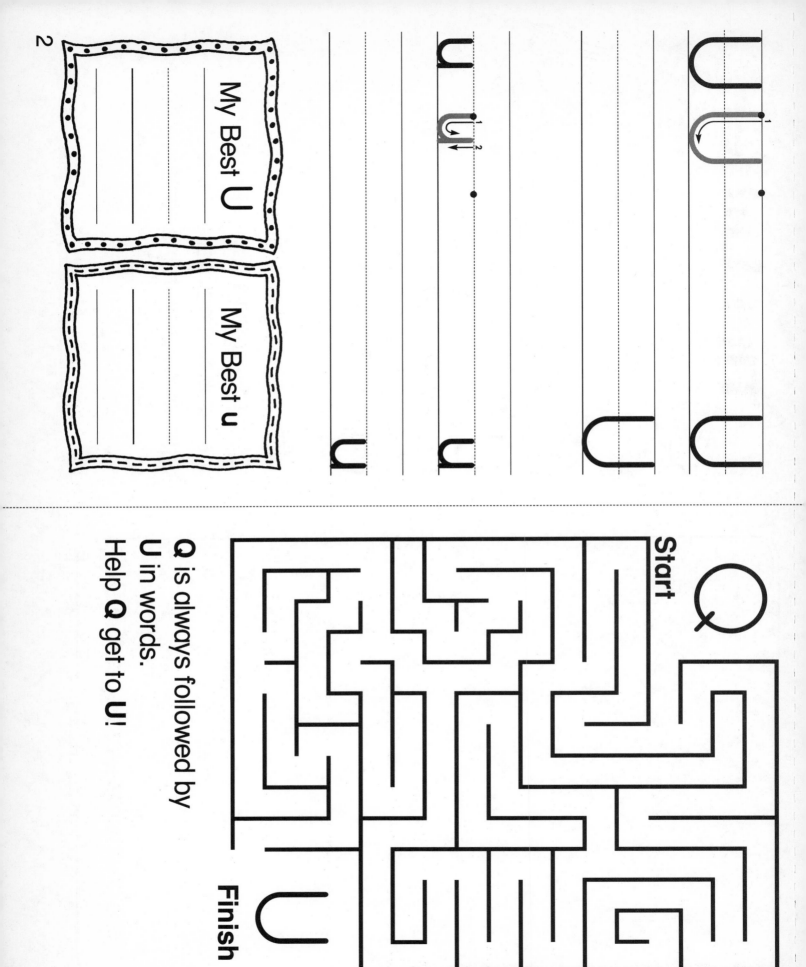

My Best U

My Best u

Q is always followed by
U in words.
Help Q get to U!

Start

Finish

The Letter Vv

Slant down first,
then up, like so.
This upside-down volcano
is ready to blow!

by _____

Here are things that begin with **Vv**!

My Best V

My Best v

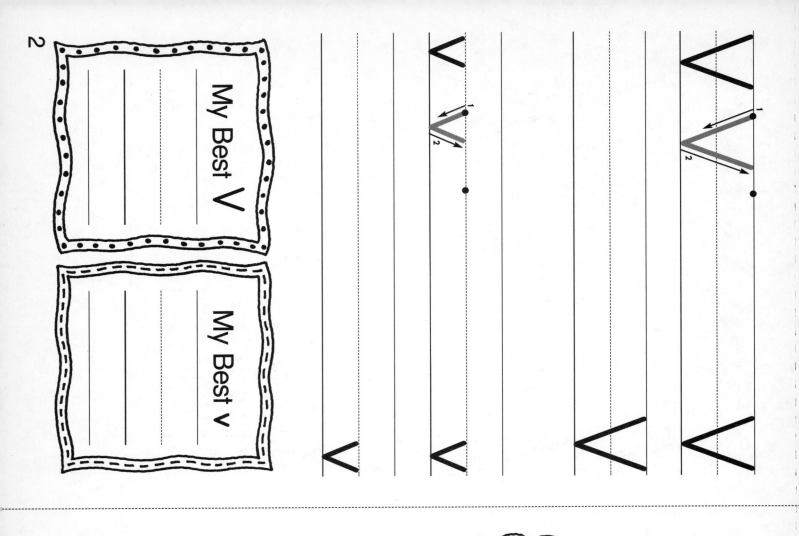

Decorate this valentine with Vv's.

The Letter

w and **w** have two pointy waves.
Swim in the water if you're brave!

by _____

Here are things that begin with **Ww**!

My Best W

My Best w

How many **Ww**'s can you
find under the water?
Circle them all.
Then color the wet scene.

The Letter

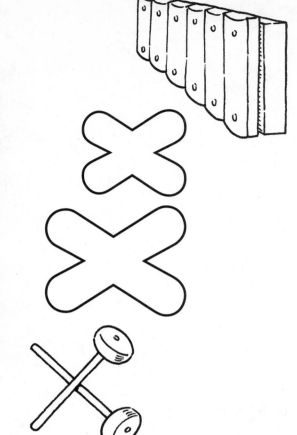

I Can Write My ABCs: Mini-Books   Scholastic Professional Books

A criss and a cross,
and in case you forgot,
where is the treasure?
X marks the spot!

by _____

Here are things that begin with **Xx**!

4

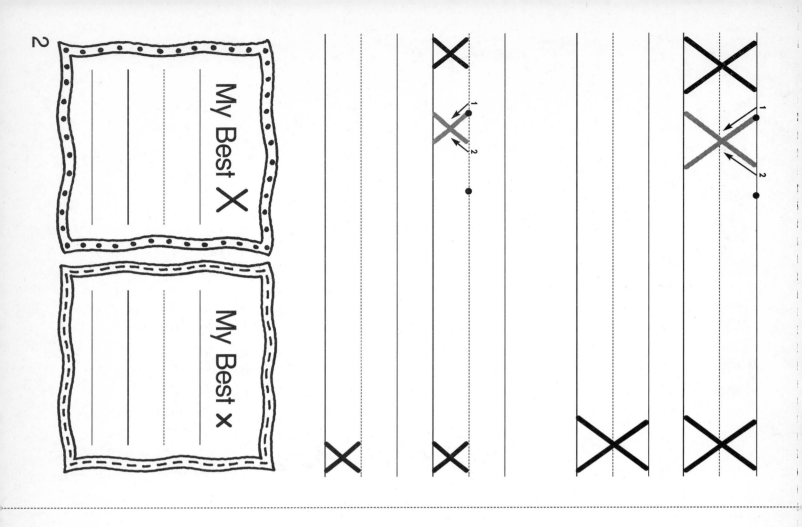

My Best X

My Best x

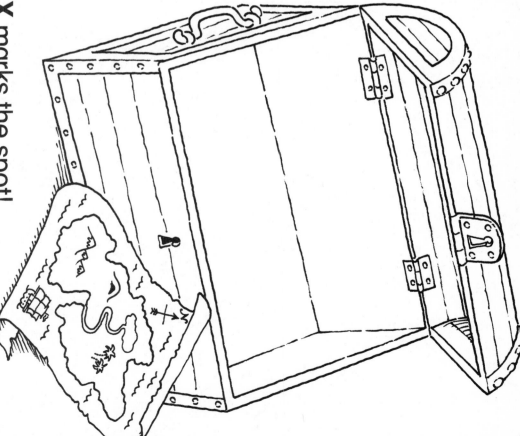

X marks the spot!
Draw your own treasure in the chest.
Where will you hide the treasure?
On the map, write an X or x to mark
the spot.

The Letter Yy

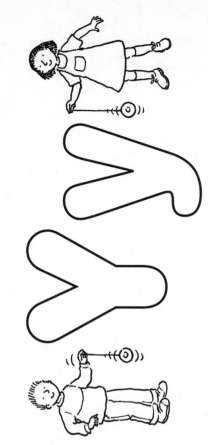

Capital **Y** has a V in the air.
The pole at the bottom holds it there.

Slant down right, down to the ground.
Slant down left,
and take it underground.

by _____

Here are things that begin with **Yy!**

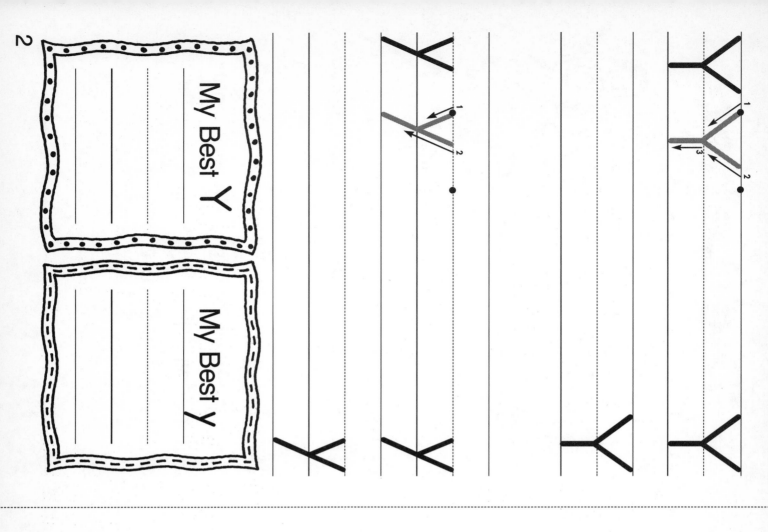

Y y

My Best Y

My Best y

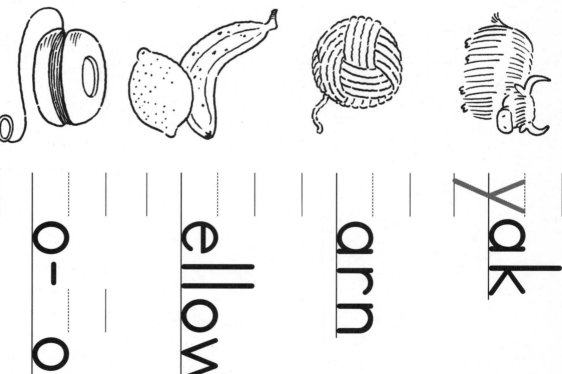

Write Y or y to finish these words.
Can you read them? Yay!

y a k

___ arn

___ ellow

___ o- o

The Letter

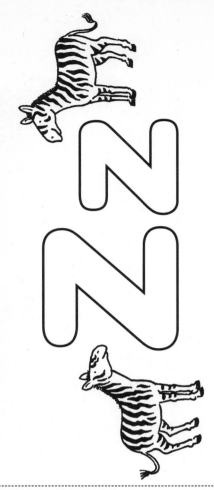

Zz

Zigzag **Z** and **z** are easy, you see.
Just zig a zag—1, 2, 3!

Here are things that begin with **Zz!**

by _____

4

4

Z Z Z

Z Z

Z Z Z

Z Z

My Best Z

My Best z

Zelda is tired. Add some **Zz**'s to show that she is sleeping.

Zz

I Can Write My ABC's!

Aa

Bb

by _____

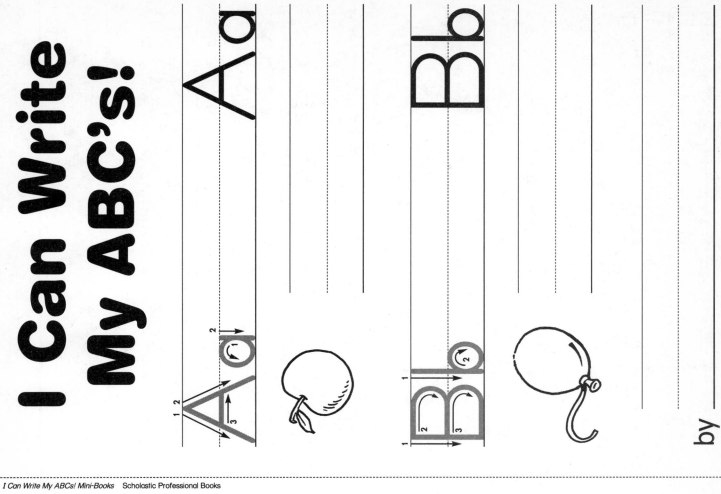

I Can Write My ABCs! Mini-Books   Scholastic Professional Books

Xx

Yy

Zz

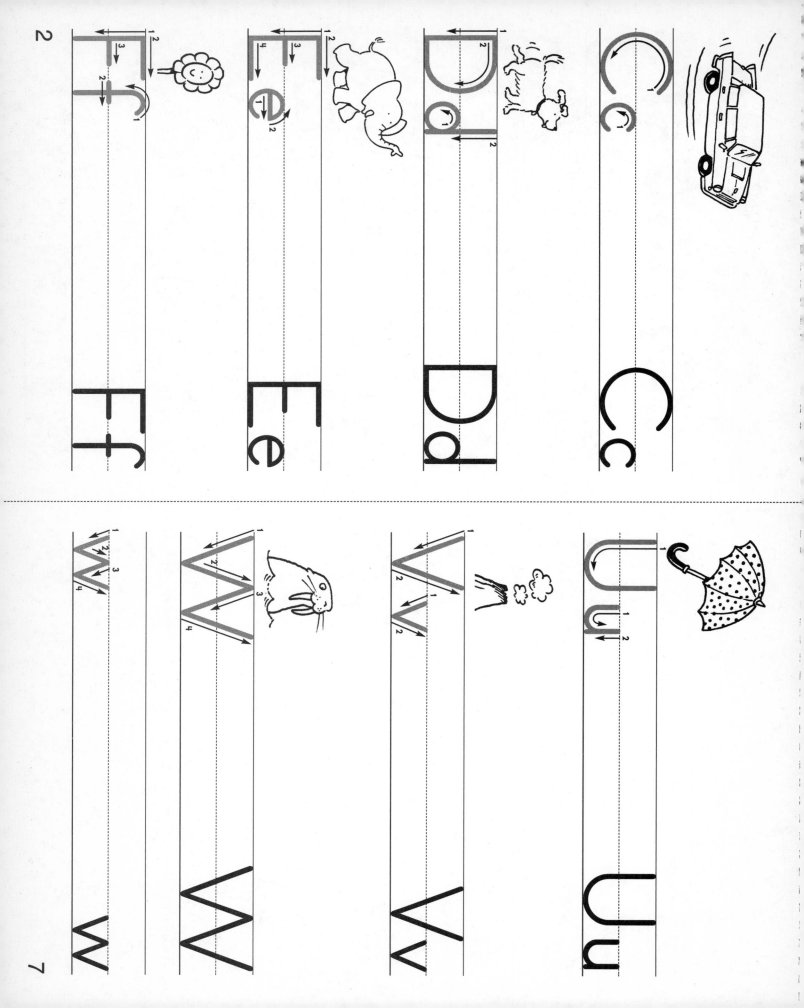

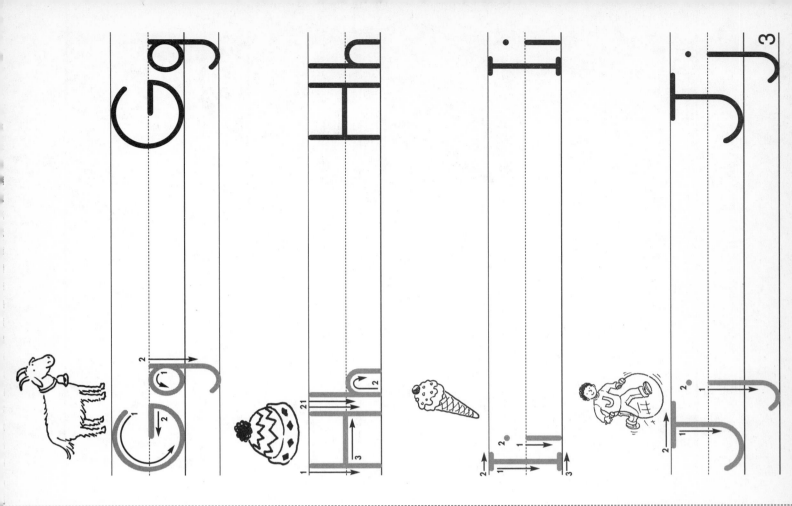

Gg

Hh

Ii

Jj

I Can Write My ABCs: Mini-Books   Scholastic Professional Books

Qq

Rr

Ss

Tt

Alphabet Books

ABC by Jan Pie'nkowski (Little Simon, 1998)

ABC by William Wegman (Hyperion, 1994)

ABC Animal Riddles by Susan Joyce (Peel Productions, 1999)

The ABC Bunny by Wanda Gag (Coward, McCann & Geoghegan,1933)

ABC Dogs by Kathy Darling and Tara Darling (Walker & Co., 1997)

ABC: Egyptian Art From the Brooklyn Museum by Florence Cassen Mayers (Harry N. Abrams, 1988)

ABC Yummy by Lisa Jahn-Clough (Houghton Mifflin, 1997)

Abracadabra to Zigzag: An Alphabet Book by Nancy Lecourt (Lothrop, Lee & Shepard, 1991)

A, B, See! by Tana Hoban (Greenwillow, 1982)

A, My Name Is Alice by Jane Bayer (Dial, 1984)

A You're Adorable by Buddy Kaye (Candlewick Press, 1994)

The Absolutely Awful Alphabet by Mordicai Gerstein (Harcourt, 1999)

The Accidental Zucchini: An Unexpected Alphabet by Max Grover (Browndeer Press, 1993)

Afro-Bets ABC Book by Cheryl Willis Hudson (Just Us Books, 1988)

Alfred's Alphabet Walk by Victoria Chess (Greenwillow, 1979)

Alison's Zinnia by Anita Lobel (Greenwillow, 1990)

All Aboard ABC by Doug Magee and Robert Newman (Dutton, 1990)

Alligator Arrived With Apples: A Potluck Alphabet Feast by Crescent Dragonwagon (Macmillan, 1987)

Alligators All Around: An Alphabet by Maurice Sendak (HarperCollins, 1962)

All in the Woodland Early: An ABC Book by Jane Yolen (Collins, 1979)

Alphababies by Kim Golding (DK Publishing, 1998)

Alphabatics by Suse MacDonald (Aladdin, 1992)

Alphabears: An ABC Book by Kathleen Hague (Holt, Rinehart & Winston, 1984)

The Alphabet From Z to A (With Much Confusion on the Way) by Judith Viorst (Atheneum, 1994)

An Alphabet of Animals by Christopher Wormell (Dial, 1990)

An Alphabet of Dinosaurs by Peter Dodson (Scholastic, 1995)

Alphabet Out Loud by Ruth Gembicki Bragg (Picture Book Studio, 1991)

Alphabet Puzzle by Jill Downie (Lothrop, Lee & Shepard, 1988)

Alphabet Soup by Kate Banks (Knopf, 1988)

Alphabet Soup by Abbie Zabar (Stewart, Tabori & Chang, 1990)

Alphabet Times Four: An International ABC by Ruth Brown (Dutton, 1991)

The Alphabet Tree by Leo Lionni (Pantheon, 1968)

AlphaTales Learning Library: 26 Paperback Books Plus Teaching Guide (Scholastic Teaching Resources, 2001)

Animal Alphabet by Bert Kitchen (Dial, 1984)

Animalia by Graeme Base (Viking, 1986)

Anno's Alphabet: An Adventure in Imagination by Mitsumasa Anno (Crowell, 1975)

The Ark in the Attic: An Alphabet Adventure by Eileen Doolittle (Godine, 1987)

Ashanti to Zulu: African Traditions by Margaret Musgrove (Dial, 1976)

Aster Aardvark's Alphabet Adventures by Steven Kellogg (William Morrow, 1987)

Baseball ABC by Florence Cassen Mayers (Harry N. Abrams, 1994)

The Butterfly Alphabet by Kjell B. Sandved (Scholastic, 1996)

C Is for Curious: An ABC of Feelings by Woodleigh Hubbard (Chronicle Books, 1990)

California A to Z by Dorothy Hines Weaver (Rising Moon, 1999)

Cat Alphabet by Metropolitan Museum of Art (Bulfinch, 1994)

Chicka Chicka Boom Boom by Bill Martin Jr. and John Archambault (Simon & Schuster, 1989)

City Seen From A to Z by Rachel Isadora (Greenwillow, 1983)

Clifford's ABC by Norman Bridwell (Scholastic, 1994)

Community Helpers From A to Z by Bobbie Kalman (Crabtree, 1998)

Crazy Alphabet by Lynn Cox (Orchard Books, 1992)

David McPhail's Animals A to Z by David McPhail (Scholastic, 1988)

The Desert Alphabet Book by Jerry Palotta (Charlesbridge, 1994)

The Dinosaur Alphabet by Jerry Palotta (Charlesbridge, 1991)

The Disappearing Alphabet by Richard Wilbur (Harcourt Brace, 1998)

Earth From A to Z by Bobbie Kalman and John Crossingham (Crabtree, 1999)

Eating the Alphabet: Fruits and Vegetables From A to Z by Lois Ehlert (Harcourt, 1989)

Erni Cabat's Magical ABC Animals Around the Farm by Erni Cabat (Harbinger House, 1992)

The Extinct Alphabet Book by Jerry Palotta (Charlesbridge, 1993)

Farm Alphabet Book by Jane Miller (J. M. Dent, 1981)

A Farmer's Alphabet by Mary Azarian (Godine, 1981)

Firefighters A to Z by Chris L. Demarest (Simon & Schuster, 2000)

The Freshwater Alphabet Book by Jerry Palotta (Charlesbridge, 1996)

The Frog Alphabet Book by Jerry Palotta (Charlesbridge, 1990)

The Furry Alphabet Book by Jerry Palotta (Charlesbridge, 1990)

From Acorn to Zoo and Everything in Between in Alphabetical Order by Satoshi Kitamura (Farrar, Straus, and Giroux, 1992)

From Letter to Letter by Terri Sloat (Dutton, 1989)

Geography From A to Z: A Picture Glossary by Jack Knowlton (Crowell, 1988)

The Graphic Alphabet by David Pelletier (Orchard, 1996)

Gretchen's ABC by Gretchen Dow Simpson (HarperCollins, 1991)

Gyo Fujikawa's A to Z Picture Book by Gyo Fujikawa (Grosset & Dunlap, 1974)

The Handmade Alphabet by Laura Rankin (Dial, 1991)

The Icky Bug Alphabet by Jerry Palotta (Charlesbridge, 1986)

It Begins With an A by Stephanie Calmenson (Hyperion, 1993)

Jambo Means Hello: Swahili Alphabet Book by Muriel Feelings (Dial, 1974)

The Letters Are Lost by Lisa Campbell Ernst (Viking, 1996)

Mexico From A to Z by Bobbie Kalman and Jane Lewis (Crabtree, 1999)

Miss Spider's ABC by David Kirk (Scholastic, 1998)

The Monster Book of ABC Sounds by Alan Snow (Dial, 1991)

Museum Alphabet by Gisela Voss and Suwin Chan (Museum of Fine Arts, Boston 1995)

My Alphabet Animals Draw Along Book by Dixie Heath (Knight, 1993)

Pierrot's ABC Garden by Anita Lobel (Golden Books, 1992)

Pigs From A to Z by Arthur Geisert (Houghton Mifflin, 1986)

School From A to Z by Bobbie Kalman (Crabtree, 1999)

The Sesame Street ABC Book of Words by Harry McNaught (Random House, 1988)

Texas Alphabet by James Rice (Pelican Publishing, 1988)

Tomorrow's Alphabet by George Shannon (Greenwillow, 1995)

26 Letters and 99 Cents by Tana Hoban (Greenwillow, 1988)

The Underwater Alphabet Book by Jerry Palotta (Charlesbridge, 1991)

United States From A to Z by Bobbie Kalman and Kate Calder (Crabtree, 1999)

Wild Animals of Africa ABC by Hope Ryden (Lodestar, 1989)

The Wildlife A-B-C: A Nature Alphabet Book by Jan Thornhill (Simon & Schuster, 1990)

The Yucky Reptile Alphabet Book by Jerry Palotta (Charlesbridge, 1989)

The Z Was Zapped by Chris Van Allsburg (Houghton Mifflin, 1987)